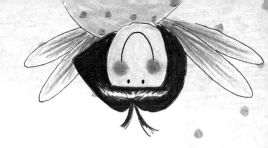

To . . . .

From . . . .

the delinquent fairy's thoughts on
aging

lauren white

SOURCEBOOKS, INC.®
NAPERVILLE, ILLINOIS

INTRODUCTION

Hello — My nAme is Flo.
AgE Doesn't boTher me :
I'm 342 aNd pRouD of it !!!
HowEver, we FaiRiEs nAturaLLy
take pRide in oUR aPpeaRaNce

aNd WORRy aBOUT SAgs, Bags, anD BloTches as much as EveryBody eLse.

SAg (!)   bAg (!!)   BlotcH (!!!)

To FiNd oUT iF you Are in Need of my ANTiAginG mAgic waNd, just Answer this simPle QUEStioN

    (simple qUEStioN)................▶

QUESTION WHICH HOBBY requiRes a loNg LengTh of STRing aNd loTs of STAmiNa?

(A) BuNgee juMping

(B) kNitting

SaDly, if KniTTiNg PoppeD inTo yoUR Head, you'RE getting inTo the dANger zoNe

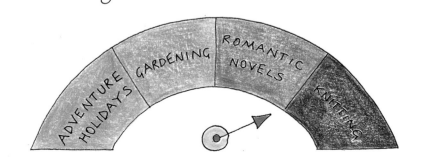

THere is A cuRe: it's cAlled
AtTituDE !!!
with it you CAN ReverSE
the SiGNs of Aging (TRust
me, I'm a Fairy!)

(dribble)

IF youR PerSoNAl fouNtAin of
youTh couLd do with some
puMping up ~ reAd oN....

THE SCIENCE BIT...

Here is a skin cell...

... they are very small...

... get a wig (nobody will notice !!!...)

Flo's

Guide To...

Choosing The dReadeD Spectacles...

perfect!

THE
WISDOM
OF
FLO

to take off ten years

change the lighting

(THE SCIENCE BIT CONT'd..)

exfoliation is the key...

FIRST SIGNS OF AGING (F.S.O.A.)...

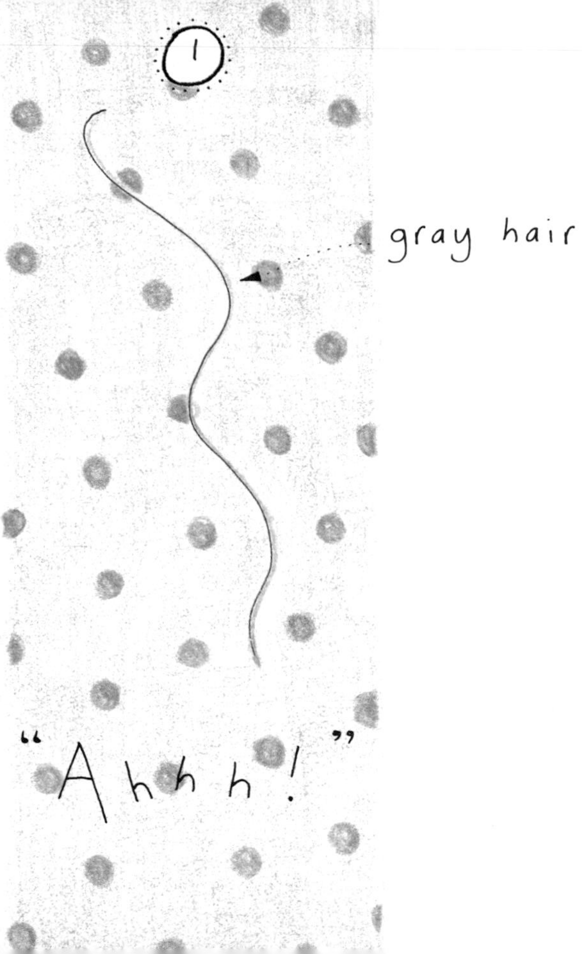

"TOO LOUD"

No Surrender
Nº 2

gravity

heavy-duty
straps

industrial strength
underwiring

double strength
"super clench"
slimline
waistband

"antigravity"
support cups

magic
tummy
flattening
panel

mega-weave
extra-strong-
buttock-firming
fabric

...lift and separate!!

Flo's "Old Trout" Kit!

dark glasses ("hide a multitude dear!"...)

Granny cardigan : with hidden pockets for
frisbees, water pistols, etc

Support stockings (will stand up on their own if necessary!)

illuminated walking stick (will double as "light saber"
in emergencies!!!)

Spring-loaded sneakers

handbag containing :

little pick-me-up : isotonic sports drink for extra stamina

kickboxing club membership

reading material : blush-making bodice ripper!

jumbo pack of hyper-mega-super-strong
mints for extra alertness

(THE SCIENCE BIT CONT'D...)

diet can have huge effects ...

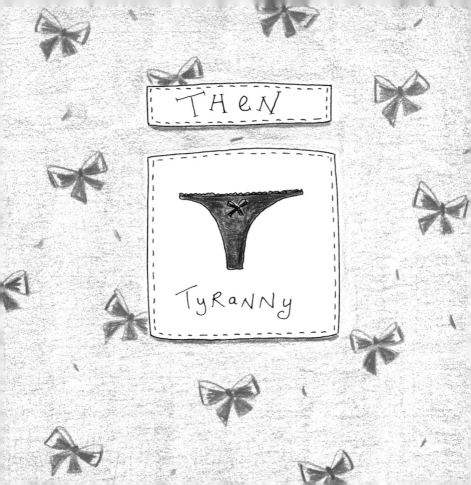

"NO SURRENDER"
Nº 3

...er.....um.....forgetfulness.....

......tie a knot in your handkerchief....

THE WISDOM OF FLO

age brings wisdom...........

. . . . . .if only you could remember it ! . . . .

THeN

TREAsuRed

Now

TREASURED

"No Surrender"
Nº 4

repeating yourself . . . .

keep making new friends!

(THE SCIENCE BIT ConT'd...)

exercise has firming effects...

CAN
YOU READ
THIS OR DO
YOU NEED A PAIR
OF SPECTACLES ?

"WHaT LEtTERS?"

DON'T say OLD, SAY......

strong .... capable

able .... learned...

sharp .... advanced .... vigorous .... practiced ....

confident .... accomplished

lively .... interesting .... vital .... bright ....

beautiful

mature ···· adult ··· blooming ··· in your prime ···· experienced

appreciated ··· thriving ··· seasoned ··· mellow

wise ····· successful ··· flourishing ···· shrewd ·· abiding

astute ···· refined ···· cultured ···· canny ··· powerful

elevated ···· supreme ···· erudite ··· influential

"No Surrender"
Nº5

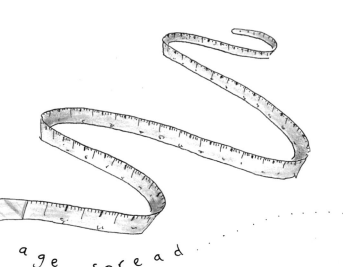

...middle age spread...

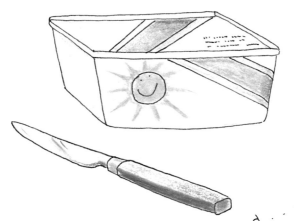

low-fat spread

THeN

ParTy Time

Now

BedTiMe!

creaking joints . . . .

...cut down on the skateboarding......

Flo's

Guide To...

Going Blonde Gracefully.....

..There comes a time when we all have to face facts!...

(THE SCiENCe BiT ConT'd...)

beware of too much sunshine ....

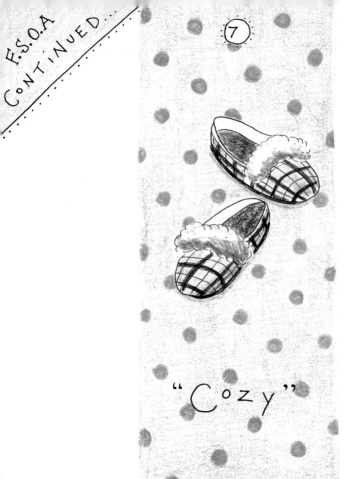

"Cozy"

"DAZZLING!"

longsightedness....

be resourceful

THE WISDOM OF FLO

the elixir of youth

...comes in all shapes and sizes.........

(.... and costs a fortune!....)

(THE SCIENCE BIT CONT'd...)

some cells are preprogrammed...

"No Surrender"
Nº 8

. . . h o t   f l a s h e s . . .

cold showers

THE
WISDOM
OF
FLO

...... if you can't read the menu..............

.......be prepared for surprises !........

THeN

PAiN

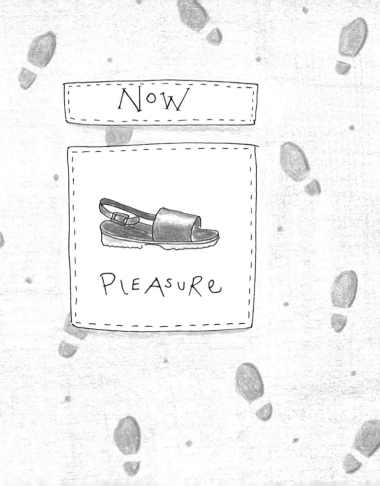

(THE SciENce BiT ConT'd...)

moisture is vital ...

THE
WISDOM
OF
FLO

feeling saggy?

Stand on your head !!!

This counteracts
gravitational
downforce ↓ ↓
↓ ↓

Flo's
Guide To...

Facial Exercises ....

..... "Ahhh" ...... "Eeee" .... "Oooh" .....

. . . . (E<u>ve</u>ry dAy, reMemBer) . . . .

. . . . . . "Aye." . . . . "Ummm" . . . . . . "Ouch!" . . .

(THE SCIENCE BIT CONT,d...)

cells respond well to pampering !...

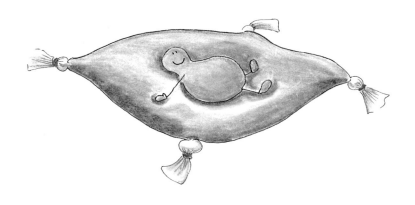

Flo's
GUIDE TO...

Trying To . . . .

. . . . um . . . . er . . . . eee . . . . .

. . . . REMEMBER ! . . .

. . . . . aw . . . . ahh . . . . . oh forget it . . .

THEN

DIET BREAKER

(THE SCIENCE BIT CONT'd...)

Sometimes, it doesn't matter what you do......

(self - destructive cell)

"No Surrender"
Nº 10

decrepitude

attitude!

REMEMBER
Age is NOT A
NumbeR —
iT's A sTATe
of Mind !

Lauren White spent much of her childhood at the bottom of the garden involved in a fruitless search for a real live fairy! Many years later, up popped Flo: Lauren comments "You imagine a shy, delicate creature with shimmering wings and a bell-like laugh—I got saddled with Flo!"

Flo has an opinion on everything. She's mischievous, subversive, and likes taking a very wry look at the antics of mortals. Lauren has managed to capture some of Flo's thoughts on aspects of the human condition and set them down in this little book.

Flo and Lauren live in the village of Cranfield in Bedfordshire, England, with Michael (mortal) and Jack (canine; terrified of Flo), where Lauren spends her spare time sketching, playing the piano, and adding to her collection of Victorian pixie lights (53 at present) by scouring antique shops and fairs. She has produced gift books celebrating life, books of spells (with Flo's guidance), and her designs for Hotchpotch greetings cards are sold around the world.

Sourcebooks, Inc.
P.O. Box 4410, Naperville, Illinois 60567-4410

(630) 961-3900
FAX: (630) 961-2168

Printed and bound in Spain

MQ 10 9 8 7 6 5 4 3 2 1

ISBN: 1-57071-637-4